I0140044

Book of Poems

God's Love, Mother's Love, Faith & Dreams

Author: Willeen Williams

God's Love, Mother's Love, Faith & Dreams

God's Love, Mother's Love, Faith & Dreams

Book of Poems

God's Love, Mother's Love, Faith & Dreams

Author: Willeen G. Williams

The Alpha Word House Publisher

God's Love, Mother's Love, Faith & Dreams

Book of Poems

God's Love, Mother's Love, Faith & Dreams

Author: Willeen G. Williams

The Alpha Word House Publisher

God's Love, Mother's Love, Faith & Dreams

The Alpha Word House Publisher

Copyright ©2017 by Willeen G. Williams

Library of Congress Cataloging in- Publication Data

Washington, D.C.

God's Love, Mother's Love, Faith & Dreams

Author: Willeen G. Williams

ISBN- 978-0-9987241-3-3

Printed in the United States of America

Book of Poems

God's Love, Mother's Love, Faith & Dreams

Author: Willeen G. Williams

The Alpha Word House Publisher

CONTENTS

A Mother's Love

A mother's love never grows cold.

A mother's love never grows old.

A mother's love grows deep from the soul.

A mother's love grows like a flower it blooms.

The stem will begin to grow, and the leaves blooms surely full of life it will prosper.

A mother' s love is a gift from above, and spoken by the Heavenly Father with his wings spread like the wings of a dove.

A mother's love is so special inside, and it will never be able to hide.

A mother's love is like the north star.

I will still love you far, and nearby my dear child.

Life Precious Moments

Precious is the time.

Real is the day.

Cool is the ocean breeze.

Ice is on the mountain top to stay.

I had opened, my mouth to inhale the fresh breath of air.

My eyes are gleaming far and near, and the precious

moments is crystal clear.

I had spent many precious moment during the break of day.

The sun has now raise in the sky, and soon another day will

go by.

Now, I have to move on cause the day is about gone.

Life has precious moments; I will always remember, and

hold on to.

Play Time

When, I was a little boy, and played with my toys.

I will always fall off my bike, and get right back up, and hold on tight.

I was always laughing, and ride until almost night.

I was jumping, skipping, riding, and sliding.

Oh, mine how time is flying.

Now, it is time to stop playing, and get ready for bed.

Soon another day is a dawning up ahead.

Good night, and soon play time will appear once again.

Spring Time Again

Spring time is in the air.

Spring will bring sprinkles and showers.

Spring will bring April and May Flowers.

Spring will bring forth flying bees.

Spring will bring forth pollen that cause me to sneeze.

Spring will bring froth green leaves on the trees.

Spring will bring forth green grass to grow on the ground.

It is time to mow my lawn now, and it is something I have to do.

I do not have much time to talk to you.

Now is the time spring has sprung, and trying to make sure all my work is done.

Distance is the shore

I am interested in learning much more

Standing by the light of day.

Time is moving right away

All the rushing sounds and movements that sends chills

right through me.

Now the sweet tones of music are playing softly in my ears,

and the distance shore is near.

The heartbeat of American, and so are the beautiful ocean

sounds, shells laying in the sand, picking them up with my

hands.

Beautiful Mountains

Sunny day it is now

Up at sunrise to see a beautiful day

Mountains are big

Mountains are smoky, and gray

Every cloud hanging low in the sky

Right in the midst it is appearing this way

The sun is hot

In my time of travel is far spent

My journey was fine

Evening has now ended, and it is time to turn in say good night.

New Journey

Crossing my path

On another journey

Up on the other side

Now it is the right time to see

The blue sky is above

Rain is failing on a hot day

Yes, it is now time for me to rest my head

Relaxing is a great thing to do

Oh, I am excited about waiting for another day to begin

Already up, I am ready to go again

Day break, its day break now the sun is shining through,

and off with a new journey to start my day.

I Will Give God Praise

God is real

He is in my heart

Rejoicing to the Glory of God

In my heart, I will praise thee

Singing unto the Lord

Trusting in the name of Jesus

My faith is in the Almighty King

All my life I will say thank you

Shall my heart continue to worship the Lord

Day and night, I will lift up Holy hands unto the Lord

All my life, I will give you praise

Yes God, you are my King of King, and Lord of Lord.

God's Love, Mother's Love, Faith & Dreams

God's Love for You

God's heart has love for you

God's heart is bigger than a flower

God's heart is bigger than the mountains

God's written word is love for you

God's loves you so much more than the world would do

God's love was proven through his own Jesus on the cross

God's love is greater, and now your soul will not be lost.

God's love for you is without any cost.

Spring Has Sprung

Grass is now growing

All ready for the new spring season

Spring has now arisen now that's a good reason

Sitting outside to enjoy my free time

In my little town is spring time to see, and enjoy

Now, I am happy and free

Getting a chance to express the real me

Right from the beginning to the ending

Every day spring is blowing my way

Every day is always time to pray

Now it is time to forget the past, and enjoy the spring while it last.

God's Love in the Winter

God's love for the winter

God's love for the blue sky

God's love for the star that shin at night

God's love is for you and I

God's love is for the winter

God's love for the frost that lays on the ground

God's love for the ice on the trees that is still hang down

God's love for the flakes that fall from the sky

God's love is for you and I

God's love for the winter

God love is when we shiver in the cold, and the snow

God's love is wrapping us up from head to toe.

The Breaking of Day

The breaking of day

 God Helping me to see my way

Every step I will pray

Bring my life a glorious fulfill day

Resting in the pleasure of God

Every lasting beauty placed on this earth

As much time is to far spent

Keeping my mind focus

In the present of King Jesus

Now it is a wonderful day

Grace has now fulfilled, beautiful and real

Day after day I will pray

All the way with a bright shiny day

You are my sunshine at the break of day, Oh Lord.

Love in My Home

After all I been through in life

A home is supposed to be filled with love

Up and down is filled with a joyful sound

Seeing every step that I will take

In the middle of the night I will awake

Smiling to see another day

All the good things God

Has brought my way

On a Jesus filled day

My home is filled with love and happiness

Every single day, God I thank for a happy home to stay.

Mother May I

Mother may I

 Say thanks for your beautiful smile

Mother may I

Say thanks for your gentle touch

Mother may I

Say thanks for sending me to school

Mother may I

Say thanks for cooking my food

Mother may I

Say thanks for combing my hair

Mother may I

Say thanks for washing my cloths

Mother may I

Say thanks for wiping my noise

Mother may I

Say thanks for praying me through rough times

Mother may I

Say thank you, and I love you.

What Life Will Bring?

All the things you have been through in life

Happy times sometime even sad moments

Open your eyes and see you are still bless

Ups and down you may go through but the love still flows

Seeing all the blessings in life God brings

Every step of the way God will bring happiness my way

In the midst life, will sometimes bring many things

Sometimes a smile in life will bring you along the way

All the good things God will bring in your life is a blessing

Hoping to bring greater smiles even while you are resting

God able to make my life joyful filled day all the way

My life is a happy, and free that is what God done for me.

Finding Love

Down to the store and out the door

You want to find love

You dash out to see will that day finally come

Now you are wondering how long will it take

You look up to the sky eyes filled with tears

God will fill your heart with his love, and joy

Now you will never have to worry about a broken heart

anymore.

By the Ocean

Standing by the ocean front

Wondering which way to turn

Evening is far spent and beautiful

Evening is filled with so much laughter

Tears are flowing down my face

Down by the ocean side standing with arms open wide

Resting in the arms of Jesus standing beside me by the

ocean side.

Hope

Hope is like a flower

Open wide filled with beauty

Pure and gentle hope is in me

Everlasting hope and dreams

There is nothing like hope to help fulfill my dreams

Bringing forth the beauty of hope blossom on the inside

Even in the midst of my busy day hope is always alive

Natural seeds are planted in the ground to grow

The hope that lies with in me has set me free

Jesus is the best hope for me.

Love

Roses are red too

The sky is blue

The stares are bright

Walking on the board walk with you tonight

My eyes are filled with gleam

Holding your hands on the board walk tonight

The night is still beautiful filled with stars in the sky

My heart is filled with love and peace forever to enjoy

God is my love for today, tomorrow, and forever more

God's love I will also hold to enjoy.

The Mountains

The peak of the tall mountains

Oh, the mountains are beautiful and free

Pure bright and smoky gray, blue, and red

Looking at the mountains are beautiful to me

The sun is shining hot down on me

A twist of the wind blowing my way

Keeping my day still beautiful anyway

Oh, the joy of watching the mountains standing tall

My heart is filled with joy through the winter, spring,

summer, and fall watching the mountains through it all.

Miracles

Sometimes miracles are big and small

In the present of my eyes I love them all

Right from the hands of the Mighty King Jesus

Arms are stretch wide open to show me he cares

Every day with Jesus is sweeter than the day before

The miracles are still flowing my way every day

Every morning that I awake that is a miracle for me to see

large or small God, I thank you for all my miracles today.

God's Love Is Still Pure

God's love is still pure

To create me and you

God's love is filled with joy

God's love is still pure

God's love will keep you strong

God's love will help you understand when things go wrong

God's pure love will never leave you alone

God's love is still pure

God love is still free

In the midst, a trouble world

We are not alone

God's pure love is still strong

No matter what keep hanging on.

Cold Winter Night

On a cold winter morn

The dew is on the ground

The rain is falling now

Late in the evening

On a cold winter night

The brisk of the cold wind is in the air

The night is still filled with hope

 My teeth are shaking from the cold

On a cold winter night

Wrapped up in my beautiful black coat

My hands are snug in my gloves

My boots are warm, and they cover my feet

Now, it is snowing ankle deep on a cold winter night.

The Silent Cry in The Morning

Laying a sleep in my bed

Laying with my pillow is underneath my head

In the midnight, there is a silent cry appear

I am hearing sounds that is trying to break my sleep

The noise gets louder, it is trying to get next to me

Finally, it has woken me up, and my eyes filled tears

Now, the morning has come my tears is no longer silent.

My tears are no longer a dream, and it is the real thing

No, silent cry in the morning God had stop by to wipe the
tears from my eyes.

God had placed all my tear drops in a bottle, and now those
tears are gone my daughter now you not alone.

God's Love, Mother's Love, Faith & Dreams

www.ingramcontent.com/pod-product-compliance
Lightning Source LLC
Chambersburg PA
CBHW070037110426
42741CB00035B/2799